Stepping Through History

TRAVEL

PEGGY BURNS AND PETER CHRISP

Wayland

Stepping Through History

Money
News
The Post
Shops and Markets
Travel
Writing

Editor: Vanessa Cummins
Series designer: John Christopher

© Copyright 1995 Wayland (Publishers) Limited

First published in 1995 by Wayland (Publishers) Limited
61 Western Road, Hove, East Sussex BN3 1JD, England

British Library Cataloguing in Publication Data
Burns, Peggy
Travel. – (Stepping Through History Series)
I. Title II Chrisp, Peter. Series III
910.9

ISBN 0 7502 1520 8

Picture Acknowledgements
The Publishers would like to thank the following for allowing their pictures to be used in this book: Lesley and Roy Adkins 7
(below); Bridgeman 9, 12 (middle); Neil Bruce 21 (above), timeline (above); Camera Press 26 (main), 27; Chapel Studios **cover**
(left), 28, 29 (below); E.T. Archive 7 (above), 8 (above); Eye Ubiquitous 12 (below), 17, timeline (middle); Robert Harding 16, 22
(below), 23 (above); Michael Holford **cover** (top), 6, 11, 12 (above), 14; National Motor Museum (Beaulieu, England) 22 (above);
Photri 21 (below), 25; Science Photo Library 18 (above); South American Pictures 8 (below), 15; Tony Stone 29 (below), timeline
(below); Topham **cover** (main), 20, 23 (below), 26 (inset); TRH Pictures 19; Wayland
Picture Library **cover** (right); Werner Forman **title page**. All maps and artwork on the contents page and pages
4, 5, 6, 11 and 13 are by Barbara Loftus.

Typeset by Strong Silent Type
Printed and bound in Italy by G. Canale & C.S.p.A., Turin

CONTENTS

WHY PEOPLE TRAVELLED

For thousands of years, people have been travellers. The first humans travelled because they were hunters, following grazing animals, and gatherers, searching for fruit, edible roots and seeds.

Below left: During the Ice Age, sea levels were much lower than today. People were able to walk from Asia to America.

The search for food took people all over the planet. From Africa and the **Near East**, 'hunter gatherers' spread to Europe and Asia. In 50,000 years BC, they crossed the sea from Asia to Australia. By 3000 BC, people had also walked from Asia to North America. At the time, the **continents** were joined by a bridge of land.

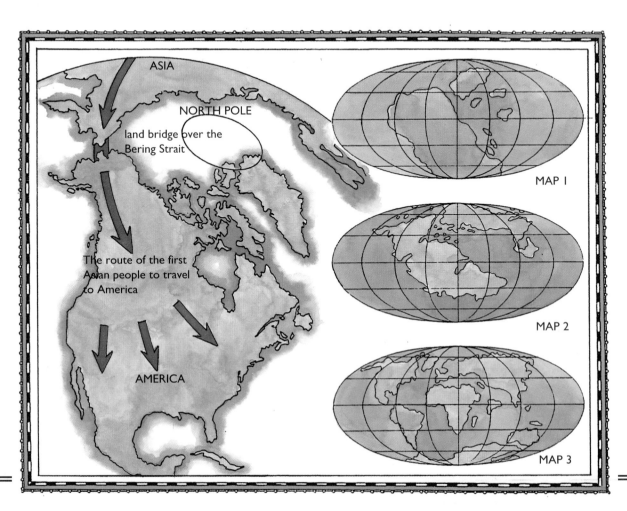

ASIA

NORTH POLE

land bridge over the Bering Strait

The route of the first Asian people to travel to America

AMERICA

MAP 1

MAP 2

MAP 3

Ten thousand years ago, a huge change took place in the way that humans lived. In the Near East, people began to grow their own food, by farming. They learned how to plant crops and to keep animals.

Later, people in other parts of the world, including South-East Asia and Central America, also became farmers. People carried on travelling but for different reasons – to find the best farming lands for their crops and animals and to settle in villages.

Left: Map 1 shows the shape of the world between 410 and 360 million years ago. Map 2 shows oceans were formed between 208 and 146 million years ago. Map 3 shows the world as it is today, which formed between 65 and 2 million years ago.

This may be the world's oldest picture of an army on the march. It was made in Turkey almost 5,000 years ago.

The wild rice plant was farmed in Asia over 10,000 years ago.

The farmers could grow more food than they needed themselves, and the extra was used to trade for tools or other goods. Craftspeople, such as weavers and potters, were therefore able to make a living. Other people travelled from village to village as traders. In time, regular trade routes were set up between different areas.

THE AMBER TRADE

One of the first goods to be traded over long distances was amber, the beautiful yellow-brown *fossil resin* from ancient trees. It was washed up on the shores of the Baltic Sea in Northern Europe and taken south overland to be traded around the Mediterranean. Baltic amber beads which are 3,600 years old have been found in Greek tombs.

The amber trade routes.

Baltic Sea
Denmark
Italy
Greece
Aegean Sea
Mediterranean

Amber deposits
Amber trade routes

A royal tomb from Mycenae in Greece.

Settled farmers stored their produce so that it could be eaten later in the year. Sometimes other people tried to steal this food, and this made the farmers very angry. This was the beginning of warfare, another reason for travelling. Some people travelled in search of rich lands to raid or conquer. Others left their homes to escape from invaders.

Farmers depended on good weather to grow their food. In a bad year, with too little rain or sun, the crops could fail. A series of bad years could cause starvation. Occasionally, there were also natural disasters, such as earthquakes and floods. All these things could set large numbers of people on the move, in search of a new home.

THE WHEEL, THE OX AND THE HORSE

The early hunter-gatherers had to travel on foot, carrying all their belongings on their backs. It was only when people began to *domesticate*, or tame, animals that they discovered an easier way of getting about.

One of the earliest animals to be domesticated was the ox, a strong, sturdy animal which is able to pull a plough or a heavy load. The ox was first used in western Asia, where people also invented the wheel. Perhaps they got the idea after using log rollers, pushed under sledges. We have no way of knowing how they did it, but they had come up with the most important invention in history.

Early wheels were heavy and made of solid wood, like this one found in Turkey.

A second-century Roman carving showing an ox pulling a cart loaded with wine.

By 3200 BC, oxen were being used to pull wheeled carts loaded with goods. We know this because we have pictures of them, from Mesopotamia (modern Iraq). They show solid wooden wheels, made in three parts and strapped together.

The next step, some time after 2000 BC, was to improve the wheel by adding spokes. The extra strength meant wheels could be much lighter in weight. The wheel was used side by side with another domesticated animal, the horse.

7

The ancient Greeks loved to race in their horse-drawn chariots. The light, spoked wheel meant that they could travel at great speed.

Horses are not strong like oxen, but they are very fast. A lighter wheel was much more important for a horse-drawn chariot than for an ox-drawn cart.

Horses and chariots had a huge impact on the way that wars were fought. People fighting on foot had no chance against a charging force of charioteers, armed with bows and arrows and spears.

In the Americas, the wheel was never used for transport, although it was used on children's pull-along toys. This may have been because American domesticated animals were all small. The largest was the llama of Peru, a distant relative of the camel. Llamas could carry packs on their backs, but they were not strong enough to pull carts.

Llamas carrying packs in Peru today.

HOW THE AZTECS TRAVELLED

The Aztecs were astonished to see Spaniards riding horses. This is Hernan Cortes, who conquered the Aztec *Empire*.

The Aztecs of Central America made all their journeys on foot or by canoe. Important people, such as the Inca emperor, travelled on litters – wooden platforms carried by slaves.

The wheel, the ox and the horse were all taken to South America by the Spaniards, who invaded Mexico in 1519. The Aztecs were terrified at their first sight of a Spaniard on a horse. They thought that the Spaniards were gods, riding on the backs of giant deer.

SAILING

The first boats were floating logs, which people could sit astride to cross rivers. They moved them by paddling with their hands or a stick, or by pushing against the river bottom with a pole. In time, they learned to tie logs together to make a raft, or they hollowed out a log to make a canoe.

Where logs were not available, people found other ways of taking to the water. In marshy countries with few trees, such as Egypt and Peru, boats were made from bundles of reeds lashed together. Other peoples, such as the Inuit of the Arctic, used animal skins stitched together and stretched over branches of trees.

The next step was to use the power of the wind to move a boat, by setting up a sail. One of the first peoples to discover sail power were the Egyptians, in about 3500 BC. At first, sailing boats were only used on the River Nile. Then the Egyptians went to sea, sailing north to the Lebanon and south to Punt (now in modern-day Somalia).

This Egyptian painting was found on the wall of an ancient tomb. It shows Egyptian sailors using oars as well as a sail. Oars were used when the wind dropped.

EUROPEAN TRAVEL

Until the 1400s, Europeans knew very little of the world. Most of their ships kept within sight of land. Then new inventions, such as the *quadrant*, made it easier for sailors to find their way at sea. They could use a quadrant to measure the height of the Pole Star. This would tell them their north-south position.

This map shows sea and river routes discovered between 1492 and 1523. Historians know this period as the Age of Exploration. Columbus, Da Gama, Magellan, Cabot, Verrazano and Cartier were all famous explorers. Cabot discovered Newfoundland (an island off the coast of Canada). Verrazano explored the River Hudson in America in 1524. Cartier explored the St Lawrence river also in America in 1535.

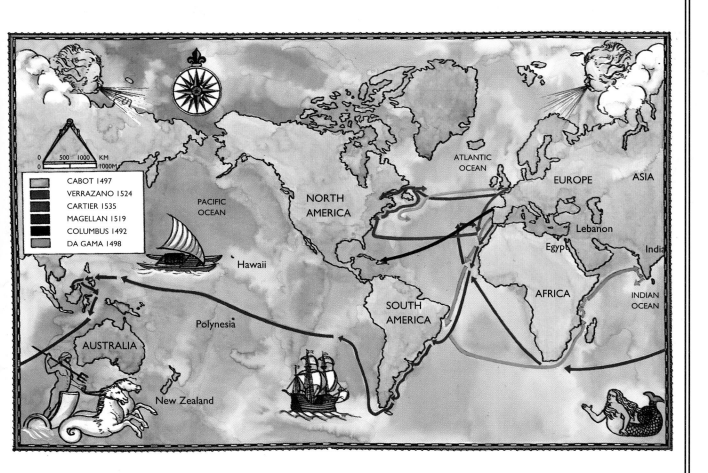

CABOT 1497
VERRAZANO 1524
CARTIER 1535
MAGELLAN 1519
COLUMBUS 1492
DA GAMA 1498

0   500   1000   KM
0   1000M

PACIFIC OCEAN

NORTH AMERICA

ATLANTIC OCEAN

EUROPE

ASIA

Lebanon

Egypt

India

Hawaii

AFRICA

INDIAN OCEAN

Polynesia

SOUTH AMERICA

AUSTRALIA

New Zealand

Between 1492 and 1522, European explorers made three voyages which later became famous. In 1492, Christopher Columbus sailed across the Atlantic to the Americas, which Europeans had no idea even existed. Six years later, Vasco da Gama found a sea route to India, by sailing south around Africa. The greatest voyage of all was made by Ferdinand Magellan, in 1519–22. One of his ships managed to sail all the way around the world.

The sextant, an improvement on the quadrant, was used at sea to measure the height of the midday sun.

POLYNESIAN SEA-VOYAGERS

The greatest sea-voyagers of all time were the Polynesians, the people who settled on islands across the Pacific Ocean between 1500 BC and AD 1000. Men, women and children travelled vast distances in open boats, together with their plants, seeds, pigs, dogs and chickens. They reached islands scattered over 20 million km², including Hawaii, and New Zealand, in the south. The Polynesians are the most widespread people on earth.

Above: A carved, Maori fishing boat. The Maori people of New Zealand are the descendants of Polynesian sea-voyagers.

Right: This girl lives in the Trobiand Islands, one of the first places to be settled by the Polynesians.

ROADS

The first roads were built by the rulers of *empires*. The Persians, the Romans and the Incas of Peru all conquered large areas of land. They built roads as a way of keeping control of the people and lands they ruled. It was vital for news to travel quickly, in case of an invasion or an uprising. It was also important for the army to be able to get from one part of the empire to another in as short a time as possible.

Below: The Incas, Romans and Persians all built roads. The Persian Royal Road stretched from Sardis, in modern-day Turkey, to Susa in Iraq. The longest road in the Roman Empire was built from Tangiers, in Morocco, to Alexandria in Egypt.

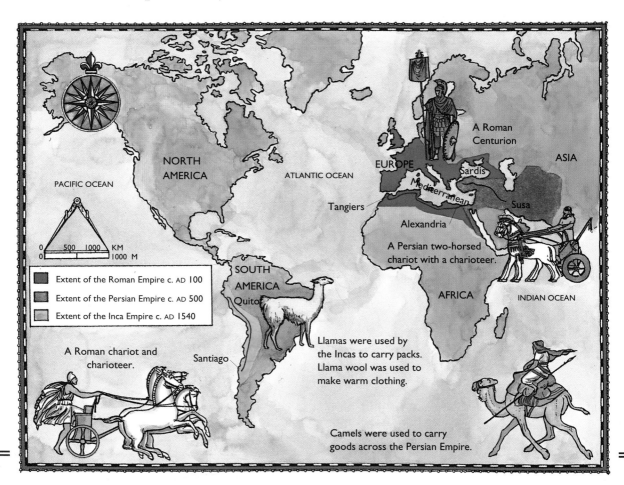

PACIFIC OCEAN

NORTH AMERICA

ATLANTIC OCEAN

EUROPE

A Roman Centurion

ASIA

Sardis

Mediterranean

Tangiers

Susa

Alexandria

A Persian two-horsed chariot with a charioteer.

0 500 1000 KM
0   1000 M

SOUTH AMERICA

Quito

■ Extent of the Roman Empire c. AD 100
■ Extent of the Persian Empire c. AD 500
□ Extent of the Inca Empire c. AD 1540

AFRICA

INDIAN OCEAN

A Roman chariot and charioteer.

Santiago

Llamas were used by the Incas to carry packs. Llama wool was used to make warm clothing.

Camels were used to carry goods across the Persian Empire.

In 500 BC, the Persians ruled a vast empire, stretching from Egypt to the edge of India. The Royal Road was 2,500 km long, from Sardis in Turkey to Susa, the Persian capital, in modern-day Iraq. It had 111 posting stations, where messengers could swap a tired horse for a fresh one. Thanks to these horses, news could travel from one end of the road to the other in just nine days.

The greatest road builders of all were the Romans, whose empire included all the lands around the Mediterranean Sea by the year 117. Previously, travellers had used winding routes. Roman roads were built to be long and straight, even if they cut through mountains or had to cross valleys with huge bridges. Today, many European roads follow roads laid by the Romans.

ROMAN ROADS

The Roman Empire lasted from 750 BC to AD 450. Roman roads were built to last; many have outlasted the empire and are still used today. The soldiers made a road by digging a trench and filling it with layers of different materials – sand, stone slabs and crushed stone – to form a cement. The top, paved with stone, curved to a crown in the middle. This helped to keep the road clear of rain water, which poured down to *drainage ditches* on either side.

A Roman road in North Africa.

A modern Inca road on a hillside in Peru. The Incas could build roads on very steep slopes.

The Inca Empire of Peru lasted from 1430 to 1525. It stretched 3,500 km from north to south and was linked up by 40,000 km of roads. Inca roads were unlike any others. They crossed deep ravines with narrow rope bridges, which swung in the wind, and they went up mountain sides using steep steps. The Incas made roads like this because they had no wheeled transport. Anywhere a person or a llama could climb, a road could be built as well.

CANALS, COACHES AND STEAM ENGINES

In the late 1700s, huge changes were taking place in Britain. The first factories were built; new machines were being invented; and industries and factories were springing up everywhere. The country was going through an 'Industrial Revolution'. All the newly produced goods needed to be transported. Britain's rivers and old, muddy roads were simply not up to it.

One of the best ways of moving goods was by *canal*. A horse can pull a much greater load on a barge than on a wagon, because the water takes most of the weight. Between 1760 and 1840, 6,500 km of canals were built in Britain.

Here, you can see the smoke rising from one of the new factories in eighteenth-century Britain. A steam train crosses over a canal. The horses that pull the barges are having a well-earned rest.

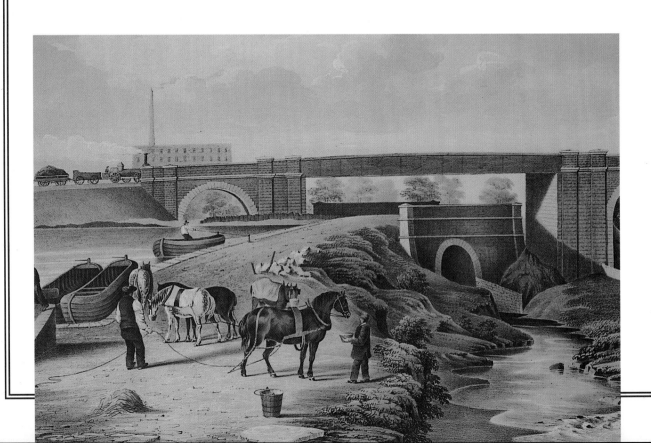

At the same time, roads were built and repaired, with money raised from tolls – fees paid by travellers. Two Scottish *engineers*, Thomas Telford and John McAdam, designed roads which were almost as good as those built by the Romans. Telford's roads had solid foundations and curved surfaces, to drain off rain and flood water. McAdam didn't bother with foundations, but he invented an efficient new road surface using stone chips.

Today, waterways and canals are still used for moving goods. These huge barges on the St Lawrence river in Michigan, USA travel between the Great Lakes of North America.

While the goods went by canal, people travelled along the new roads in horse-drawn coaches. Journey times became much shorter. In 1745, it took two weeks to travel from London to Edinburgh on the old roads. By 1796, using the new roads, it only took two and a half days.

The biggest change of all was brought about by a new invention, the steam engine. Coal was used to heat water in a boiler. Steam from the boiling water moved pistons, which pushed a beam or turned a wheel. At first, steam engines were only used to pump water out of mines. Then, in 1804, an engineer called Richard Trevithick built a steam engine that ran on rails.

For the first time in history, people could travel faster than a running horse. Many found the idea terrifying. They thought that they could not survive at such a high speed. Another worry was the fact that the boilers on early engines often exploded. Despite these worries, the age of the train and the steamship had arrived.

Newcomen's steam engine worked by heating water inside a cylinder (1). This pushed up a piston (2), which was balanced by a weight (3).

THE AGE OF STEAM

In 1825, the engineer George Stephenson built the world's first public railway, between the towns Stockton and Darlington in England. It was a success and wealthy people rushed forward to *invest* money in the new steam engines. By the 1840s, the whole of Britain was linked by railways.

Stephenson also designed and built steam engines to sell abroad. Soon, railway lines were being built all over the world. In Europe and Asia, they were made to link towns and cities which already existed. In the USA, the railways were built first and the towns and cities were built afterwards along the same route.

The Locomotion No. 1, built in 1825 by George Stephenson's son and partner, Robert. The engine pulled trains for more than twenty-five years.

This was the period when millions of Europeans travelled to the USA to find a new life. There were Italian, Scottish and Irish people, escaping from poverty, and Jews from eastern Europe, escaping from persecution. They crossed the Atlantic Ocean on steamships. From the east coast of the USA, many of them travelled west on trains. In 1869, the coasts of the USA were linked by rail.

The steam engine was the world's most popular form of transport until the late 1930s. Then, new ways of powering trains, such as diesel and electricity, began to take over. These were cleaner and more efficient. In the USA and Europe, they gradually replaced steam. Even so, in many parts of South America, Africa and Asia, the old steam trains are still running today.

THE FASTEST TRAIN IN THE WORLD

Today, the fastest trains in the world are the electric high-speed trains of France and Japan. These are *streamlined* and pointed at the front, so that they fly through the air like a bullet. They need specially built tracks, which are as smooth, flat and straight as possible. On a French high-speed train, you can travel 400 km in just two hours.

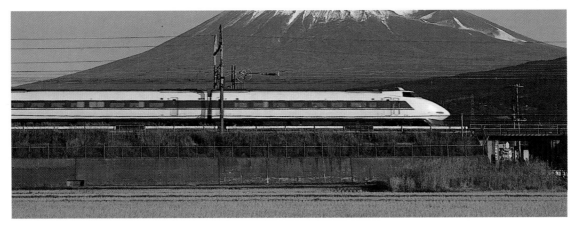

A bullet train travelling at speed in Japan.

THE FIRST CARS

Steam engines burn fuel outside the engine itself. This makes them big and heavy and only suitable for large vehicles such as trains and ships. It also takes time to start a steam engine. The coal has to be burning for a couple of hours before there is enough steam to make the engine move.

In 1859, a new kind of engine was invented which burned fuel inside. It was called the *internal combustion* (inside burning) *engine*. The first ones ran on coal gas and were used to turn factory machinery. These new engines could be much smaller than steam engines, and they were ready to start turning wheels in a very short time.

A French steam car from 1885. Steam cars were not popular because they were slow and covered the passengers in soot!

The first petrol-driven car, invented in Germany by Gottfried Daimler, looked like a carriage without horses. Together with another designer, Karl Benz, he eventually built a car which could reach a speed of 18 km per hour. At the time, this seemed amazingly fast. In Britain, cars were only allowed to go at walking pace. By a law of 1878, someone had to walk in front with a red flag, warning horse-riders to get out of the way.

An internal combustion engine, built by Gottfried Daimler in 1879.

SIEGFRIED MARCUS

The first car built by Siegfried Marcus.

Siegfried Marcus from Austria, was one of the first to try out the new internal combustion engine on a vehicle. He built a car and, in 1875, drove it around Vienna. It was so noisy and smelly that the police banned it from the roads. In 1950, the same car was taken on a trial run and was found to be still in perfect working order.

At first, only the richest people could afford cars. But in 1908, in the USA, Henry Ford brought out the Model T, a car which was easy to put together in factories.

The famous Ford Model T.

Compared to other cars, the new Model T was cheap and it sold in huge numbers. Over nineteen years, more than 15 million 'Tin Lizzies', as they were nicknamed, rolled out of Ford's factories. The Model T made motoring popular.

INTO THE AIR

For thousands of years, people have looked up at the birds in the air and dreamed of being able to fly. There are a number of stories of people who tried to fly by copying birds. They tied feathered wings to their arms and jumped off towers and cliff-tops. But no matter how hard they flapped their wings, they crashed to the ground, landing in a heap of broken bones.

Do you think this pedal-powered machine has any chance of leaving the ground?

FLIGHTS OF FANCY

Leonardo da Vinci, a fifteenth-century Italian artist and scientist, was fascinated by the idea of flight. He designed a flying machine with turning blades, like a helicopter, and another with flapping wings. Although cleverly designed, Leonardo's machines could never have worked. They relied on muscle power, and human muscles are simply not strong enough to keep a flying machine up in the air.

This wooden model is based on Leonardo's drawing of a flying machine.

It was not until the eighteenth century that people left the ground for the first time, using balloons. They were filled with hot air or hydrogen, a gas that is lighter than air. The first hot-air balloons were made in France, by Jacques and Joseph Montgolfier. They made a test flight in September 1783, sending up a cockerel, a duck and a sheep as passengers. When this was successful, they sent up a balloon with people on board.

In 1852, a French engineer, Henri Giffard, fitted a steam engine to a balloon and made the first *airship* – a balloon which could be steered. A German businessman, Count von Zeppelin, started an airship passenger service in 1910. People could travel in great luxury on Zeppelin's airships, eating fine meals and enjoying the view.

The problem with the early airships was that hydrogen could easily explode. On 7 May 1937, the Zeppelin Hindenburg burst into flames as it approached its landing in New Jersey, USA. All thirty-five people on board were killed.

The Montgolfiers' balloon, about to take off in Paris with its first passengers in 1783.

AEROPLANES

The first aeroplanes, built in the 1840s, were gliders which had no engine. Many attempts were made to add engines to gliders, but they never managed to stay in the air for more than a couple of seconds. This was because people were using steam engines, which were either too heavy or not powerful enough.

Wilbur Wright demonstrates one of his early aeroplanes in France in 1909.

The problem was solved by the Wright brothers, Orville and Wilbur, of North Carolina, USA. They built an aeroplane with two propellers, driven by a new, light internal combustion engine. On 17 December 1903, the 'Flyer', with Orville at the controls, was shot into the air by a *catapult*. Orville stayed airborne for twelve seconds, long enough to make it the first powered flight. By the end of the day, the aeroplane flew for a whole minute.

Soon, other flyers were testing their own light aeroplanes, and making longer and longer trips. On 25 July 1909, a French pilot called Louis Blériot, flew across the English Channel. Charles Lindburgh, an American, made the first solo Atlantic crossing in 1927, spending thirty-three hours in the air. There were women flyers too, including Amelia Earhart and Amy Johnson. In 1930, Amy Johnson flew all the way from Britain to Australia.

The two world wars, of 1914–18 and 1939–45, led to improvements in aeroplane design. Scientists in Germany, Britain and the USA all worked to make faster and better war planes. One result was the *jet engine*, invented by German scientists in the late 1930s. The jet engine burns fuel producing a stream of hot gases. This stream shoots backwards, pushing the aeroplane forwards. A jet engine is much faster than *propellers*.

Like many early flyers, both Amelia Earhart and Amy Johnson (inset) died in air crashes.

ROCKET POWER

Like jets, rockets use the backward thrust of burning fuel. The difference is that they carry their own oxygen with them, so they can be used in space. In 1969, the USA used rocket power to send men to the moon. Neil Armstrong and 'Buzz' Aldrin became the first humans to set foot there. Rockets have also sent *space probes* to photograph distant planets.

The Apollo 11 rocket takes off for the moon in 1969.

TRAVEL TODAY

Modern travel is fast and easy. A flight from London to New York in Concorde takes three hours and fifty minutes. Yet only 150 years ago, the same journey across the Atlantic, made by steamship, took between thirty and thirty-six days. Aeroplanes have made our world seem like a much smaller place.

Concorde can fly faster than the speed of sound. It can only carry 128 passengers which makes it expensive to run.

We have come a long way since people first learned to harness an ox to a cart. Even so, in many parts of the world, travellers still get about in traditional ways. In South America, for example, the descendants of the Incas still use llamas to carry their goods to market. Arab traders still sail across the Indian Ocean on dhows – boats made from teak or coconut planks, the design of which has not changed in more than a thousand years.

Cities all over the world have problems with traffic jams. This one is in Thailand.

In the past, travel was usually expensive. Until the 1950s, trips abroad were mainly taken by the rich. Most people had no idea of what foreign countries were like. This has all changed, thanks to cheaper flights. More people travel abroad today than ever before.

As well as the aeroplane, the car has had a huge effect on modern life. Car-owners have the freedom to travel whenever they want to. People who don't have cars depend on the lorries that bring food and other goods to the shops. Businesses rely on lorries for deliveries of raw materials and products. It would be hard to imagine life without motor vehicles. However, they also cause terrible *pollution*, particularly in cities. So many people now drive that the traffic often grinds to a halt.

The air fills with poisonous fumes, such as carbon monoxide. Governments build more and more motorways and roads to ease the flow of traffic, but the new roads simply fill up with more cars.

Cars and aeroplanes are just two examples of the many forms of transport available to us today. Somewhere, at this moment, people are travelling under the oceans in submarines. Others are crossing the water on hydrofoils and hovercrafts. In the city, cyclists are weaving their way through the traffic while, beneath them, underground trains are moving. Meanwhile, someone else is jumping off a hillside while gripping a hang-glider. At the seaside, windsurfers are racing across the waves. How many other types of transport can you think of?

Donkey-power is still important in Spain.

TIMELINE

50000 BC The first people settle in Australia.	**30000 BC** People cross from Asia into North America across a land bridge.	**8000 BC** People become farmers, in the Near East – Israel and Mesopotamia (modern Iraq).	**4400 BC** Horses are first ridden, in southern Russia.	**3500 BC** Sails used on boats on the River Nile, in Egypt.

3200 BC Wheeled carts pulled by oxen are used in Mesopotamia (modern Iraq).	**2000 BC** Sails are used on seagoing ships, by Greek sailors in the Aegean.	**106 BC** The 'Silk Roads' are opened, providing the overland trade routes between China and western Europe.		**AD 1430** The Incas build roads in South America throughout their Empire.

1492 Christopher Columbus sails across the Atlantic.		**1522** The *Victoria* captained by Magellan becomes the first ship to sail all the way around the world.	**1712** Thomas Newcomen invents the first steam engine, for pumping water.	**1783** First flights by a hot-air balloon, in France.

1804 Richard Trevithick builds a steam engine that runs on rails.	**1863** First underground railway opened, in London, England.	**1869** A railway is opened between the east and west coasts in the USA.	**1885** Gottleib Daimler makes the first four wheeled, petrol-powered car.	**1903** Orville Wright makes the first powered flight in a plane, in North Carolina, USA.

1909 Louis Blériot flies from Britain to France across the English Channel.		**1939** First jet engine is used to power an aeroplane, in Germany.	**1969** US astronauts walk on the moon.	**1990** French high speed trains reach 550 km per hour.

GLOSSARY

Airship A balloon fitted with an engine so that it can be steered. Modern airships use helium, which is much safer than explosive hydrogen.

Canal A waterway, made by people, to transport goods in barges.

Catapult A machine using levers and ropes to launch an aeroplane, or a forked stick and piece of elastic for shooting small stones.

Continents Landmasses of the world. There are seven including Africa and Australia.

Domesticate To tame, or control, animals and to breed them.

Drainage ditches Dug-out areas beside roads and fields which collect water.

Empire A large area of land, including different peoples, ruled by a single state.

Engineers People who design and make engines and machines.

Fossil resin Amber is the remains of sap from conifer trees (called fossil resin) which has been preserved over a long time.

Internal combustion engine A machine used to generate power which burns fuel inside its workings.

Invest To lend money to a scheme in order to receive more money back in the future when a profit is made.

Jet engine An engine powered by a stream, or jet, of hot gases.

Near East The lands on the east of the Mediterranean Sea, including Syria, Iraq and Turkey.

Pollution Anything that spoils the air, soil or water around us.

Propellers The part of an aeroplane or ship which rotates and makes the aeroplane fly or ship move.

Space probes Satellites which are launched into space and used to send messages.

Streamlined Designed for great speed by giving the least resistance as possible to air or water. Blunt-shaped objects give alot of resistance and sharp, curved objects give the least resistance.

BOOKS TO READ

Eryl Davies, *Transport on Land, Road and Rail,* Franklin Watts (Timeline series)1993

David Jefferies, *Flight, Flyers and Flying Machines,* Franklin Watts (Timeline series), 1993

Eric Kentley, *Boat,* Dorling Kindersley (Eyewitness Guides), 1992

Robin Kerrod, *Transport,* Wayland, 1991

Andrew Nahnm, *Flying Machine,* Dorling Kindersley (Eyewitness Guides), 1990

PLACES TO VISIT

National Aviation Museum
P.O. Box 9724, Terminal T
Ottawa, ON K1G 5A3, Canada

Scienceworks Museum
2 Booker Street
Spotswood, VIC 3015
Australia

National Railway Museum
Leeman Road
Yorkshire YO2 4XJ, England

INDEX

Numbers in **bold** indicate subjects shown in pictures as well as in the text.